AF618929

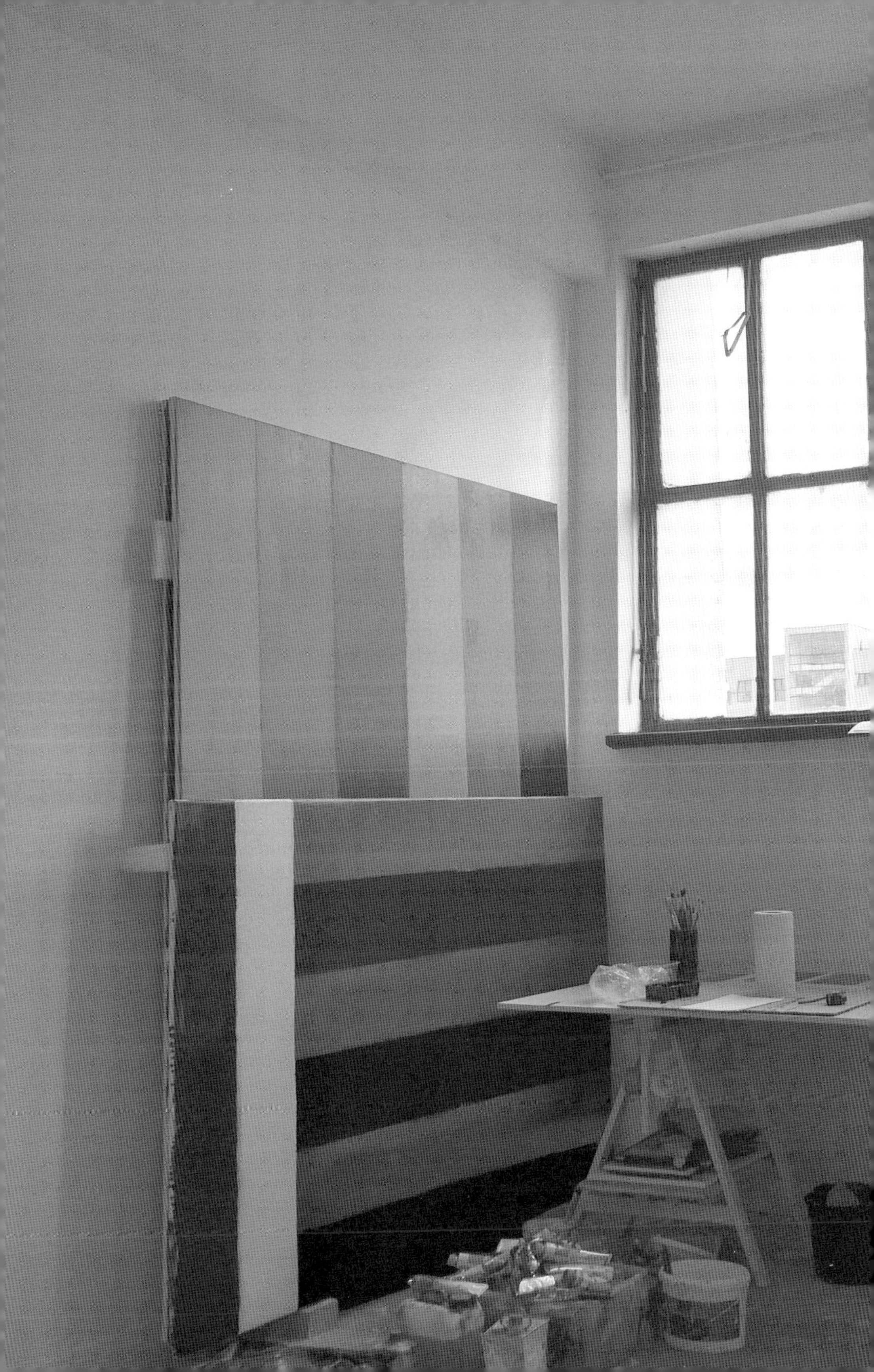

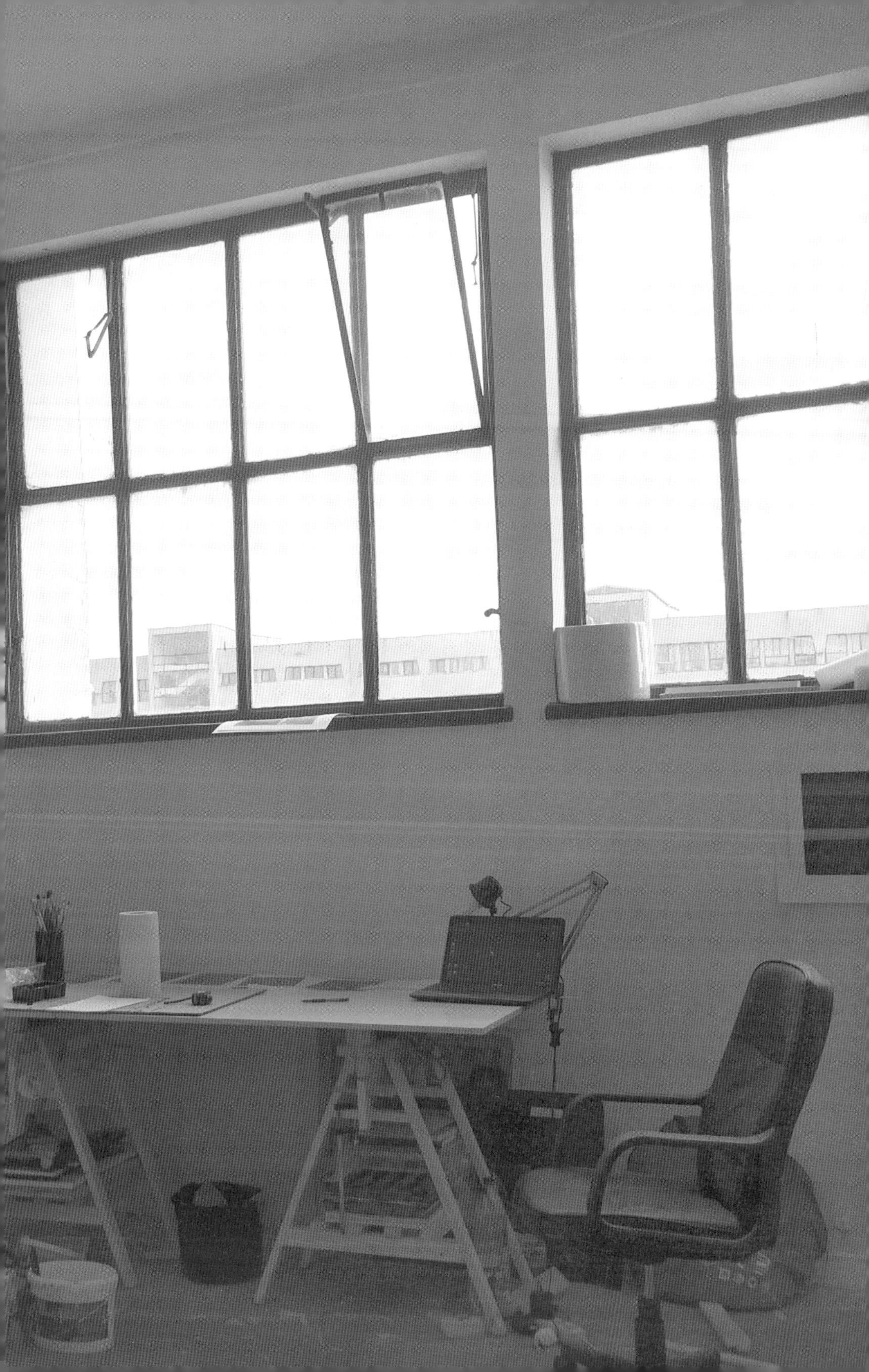

Maxim Liulca

DISTANZ

Perhaps

Sorin Neamțu in dialogue with Maxim Liulca

SN: I wonder why one feels the need for text in a catalogue...

ML: Hmm...

SN: It's a question that one inevitably comes across. Aren't images enough?

ML: Allright, but it's not a text that explains the images (or painting), but rather a text that is somehow related to the images. Of course, I do not need a word before the image, because I am the word, in fact I am the image and the word, to me it's clear. But yes, for others words might help... It's not that the image would need text, the image does not need text, the image (painting) by definition lies outside the logic of words. Where the image starts, the word stops. A word is a word, a spot of color is a spot of color, it's not a relation of "needing". And yet, in the end, language is the most advanced and intelligible way of communication. But again, not a text in the sense of description, or the explanation of the painting, but rather the poetry leading up to the painting, which includes everything up to the painting, to the image. And you know how it is, we can do the same thing - the same thoughts, feelings that we reformulate, that we recondition - but for different reasons, depending on the context, on the life of each of us. It's the same painting (apparently), but what made you do so differs from what made me do the same. And here words can be helpful.

SN: In the sense that you do not necessarily resemble others in this abstract painting.

ML: Anyway abstract painting, abstract is not a movement (such as Fauvism or Cubism), it may be a period (I think Donald Judd spoke of this at one point) like the Renaissance, the Baroque, but we cannot catalog it until it is over. And anyway, the term "abstract" is very vague. It's more a state of mind, a way of thinking. I do not know, it's not a study of shape and color. For me, colors and shapes are limited, I am very clear in color and composition, in the architecture of the image.

SN: And when you start painting, you know exactly what the composition will be, you start with a sketch, right?

ML: Yes, if not with a sketch, I have it in my mind anyway, I know the color, the shape... I have a clear idea of how a painting should look like, a painting of mine: color, composition, a more or less pre—defined set, without experiments (like if I cut a canvas using a cutter or I burn it... I don't care much about those), so somehow this part of the architecture of the image is very clear to me. Yet this clarity is at the level of an idea, somehow abstract, that is, on canvas it can be formulated and reformulated differently. And of course I have my preferences, my influences - how much I may not want to be in nature, the fact that I live in history. What I am doing now is due to what happened yesterday ... "everything that is new is therefore traditional" (I have probably heard it many times, but I think if I had not thought about it before, I would not have heard it, I remember a character from a Godard movie that said T.S. Eliot said it). It happened to me to make a painting, after that a second painting, a third, a fourth, a fifth... After that you make another that's like the first one, without realizing... it's something that has to do with a return, with a déjà vu, the present that you perceive as the past, but still present; it has the mark of the present. Okay, this is a very particular example, but it can also be used generally on a historical level. In the end, the artist is the one who reveals the meaning and essence of things. And yes, the compositional form is a simple one that has nothing to hide, which does not even need to be read in some way, has no beginning or end, it's a whole. But see, I am not interested in studying form and color, I did not care to make a thousand paintings with a thousand possibilities in color and form. Somehow the analytical part of the process is minimal, at this level I don't feel like exploring.

SN: Okay, if you know the composition, if you know the color, what makes you happy or not with the painting in the end?

ML: I should like it.

SN: Well, then if your work as a painter has a predefined color composition, what is your drive, how do you put in color, materiality? What seems to me very particular to your painting is that it is beyond composition and color choice, color palette etc. It seems to me that things happen often materially in the way you rub the canvas and in the accident. Here I find the key somehow... and how much this whole materiality thing matters.

ML: Yes, that's exactly where it all happens - but only in the end, there is also a middle - all that can be seen... But again, this pertains to the physical side of the world, the earth - and therefore in a way it offers visual joy - and in the end it's something that is not up to me, "through me" but not up to me, a movement that leads to another movement, like walking, like writing (I mean writing as a signature, writing, calligraphy) without controlling it in a way, almost instinctively. Art is not the object, art is the experience (many have said and others will say, but I have heard it in J. Albers) and the subject of my painting is the pigment... this earth, being humans that's what we are, flesh and blood. This is all that remains, that remains physically after an experience, after a day in the studio - the object (which is actually this materiality) is the exteriorized part of the act - a form of matter with a force of its own, and which did not previously exist. And if a painting gets scratched or has dust on it, that is time, that's actually "time" ("dust is the body of time"). It's that trace thing. What is art? It's a trace. We're all wearing out our soles a little. And that's not about space, it's about time. I'm more curious about time than about space. And it is not about how much materiality counts in painting either, I mean, it's a little absurd in fact... Actually this materiality is what you see, that is, an aesthetic experience... This is what painting itself is, just like music is sound, poetry is language. As Brodsky said in an interview, I do not remember the exact words, but the meaning is that, in the end, what resists, what is left is art - in his case poetry - that has to do not with society, not with the public, but with language. But here too we come to the idea of the artist's relationship with the public, which in fact does not exist, at least not directly... But that's something else. This part of the exteriorization at the material level is somewhat passive; it is related to the DNA of the painting. But again, to track back a little... when you say how much materiality counts in a painting... I also think how much the object matters, which, as you said, is part of a metaphor, is an end, a materialization of something, of the thoughts, the physical state of art. And it's not a trace, a poet's poem is also a trace, but they cannot be touched. I refer to physicality as such. And I think there's a need for that... it's just touching via the eyes. So, in the end, that's the essence, a spot (which does not talk about anything, it's not descriptive). Again, aesthetics before ethics. As small children, we perceive everything aesthetically (the lips, the mother's eyes, at two months old a child perceives them like that). The rest comes later.

SN: But my question was somewhat different; I was trying to quantify what makes a good painting, that was actually the question... I think it does not mean a specific control over the surface, but on the other hand you have chosen a composition that means a certain proportion of things in relation to the frame... that is, the composition, the ratio of the surfaces with the large surface, that is with the painting frame. Then you choose the colors, which usually are not many in your case, and are generally conversing with one another, in the sense that you have two, maximum three colors, and generally you don't combine them. And they work as entities in dialogue.

So, yet with this data, you have the feeling that this painting is defined before you start it, you know some very precise coordinates and yet that painting may be good or bad at the end, after two hours of work, and my question was what makes this thing happen?

ML: I don't know, you see. We have our criteria on how it should or how it should not be. In my case, on the part that is physically, materially, I want to be in some way and not in some other... I don't know, it feels, it's honest. You somehow have control in general, but in particular you don't. Even if you have a set-up in advance – which is in fact in anything you do, and it's a matter of history, of archiving – the more you deepen, the more you have to do with something universal, with DNA. This part of the aesthetic, somehow, leaves no room for doubt. You may have doubts whether you like it or not, but when you like it, you know it's good. "Aesthetics is the mother of ethics", I heard from Brodsky, but certainly others have said it, too. You know, it's about nature, not history. Yes, and this, the object gives you joy, makes you feel good at the end of the day... And the fact that art can be different from one person to another... Art cannot be something else, the art object can be different.

SN: But, for example, have you ever been tempted to make monochromes, to use one red in one painting?

ML: Yes.

SN: And yet you feel the need to talk. We are usually accustomed to formulating ideas by words; it is the most intelligible language. But from your point of view ideas could be pictures.

ML: I do not know, maybe ideas should not be images and vice versa. Everybody has their power and reason for being, this point needs to be found.

SN: Being a painter, you express yourself through images, not words, and I was wondering if communication through images would be possible.

ML: Yes, I don't know. It's another kind of communication. In fact, we all communicate in images very unconsciously, as I said before. And we actually started to communicate in pictures before the words...

SN: Why couldn't you use in a catalogue poetry or lyrics that you like, instead of text? Just as you illustrate a book, it's the reverse process, illustrate a catalogue with words, the words of others. To put things together in a paradoxical way. Show your vulnerabilities.

Paintings

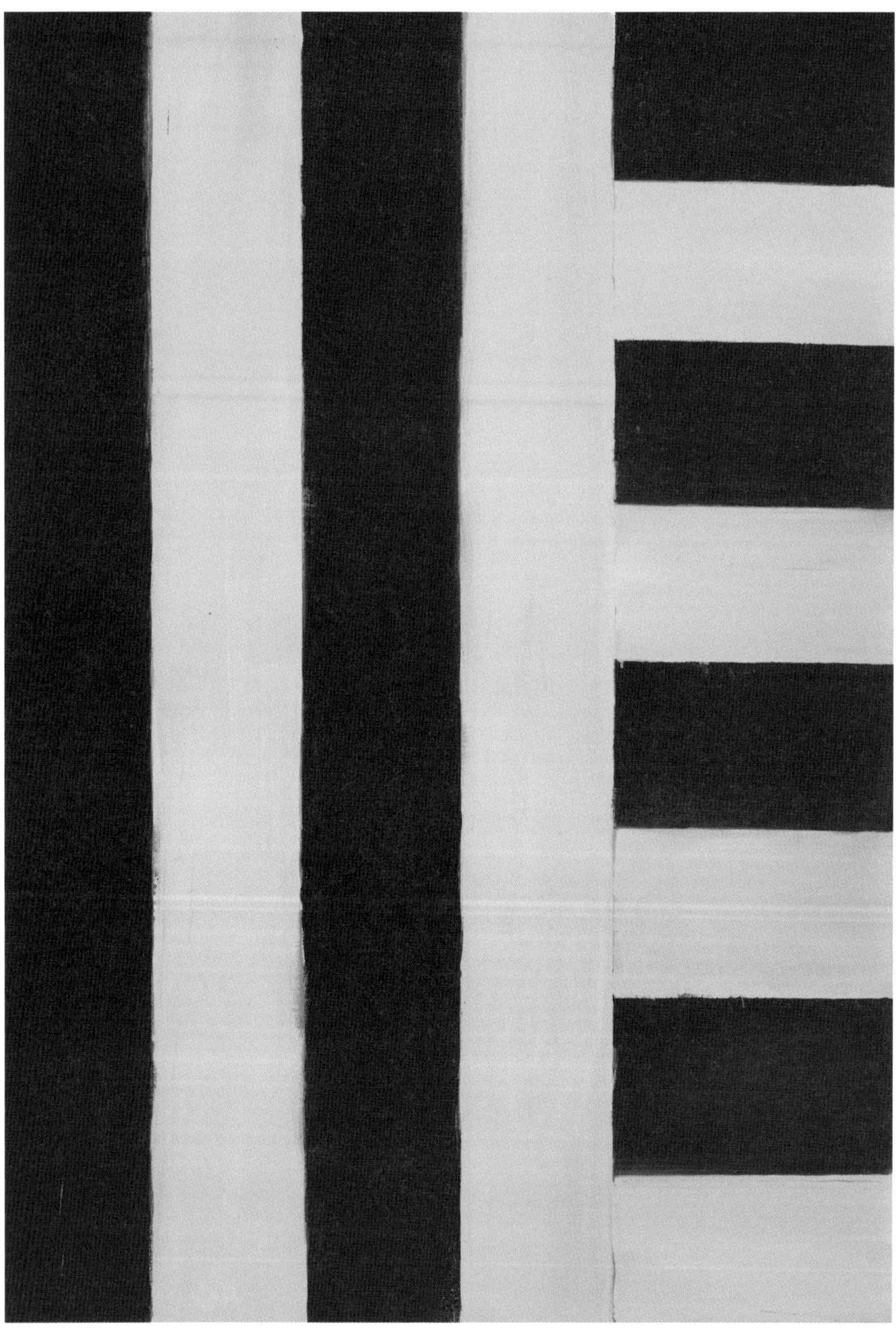

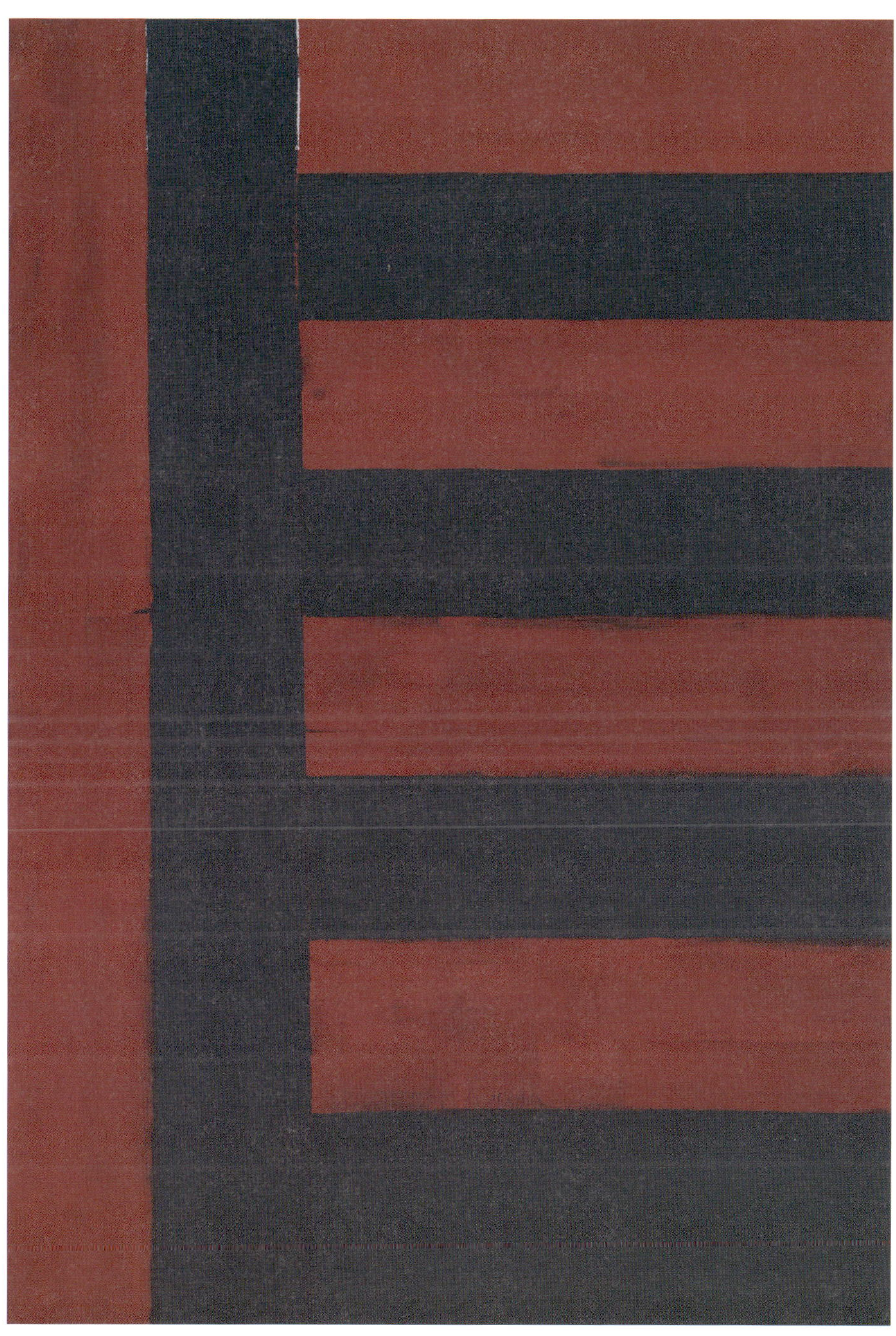

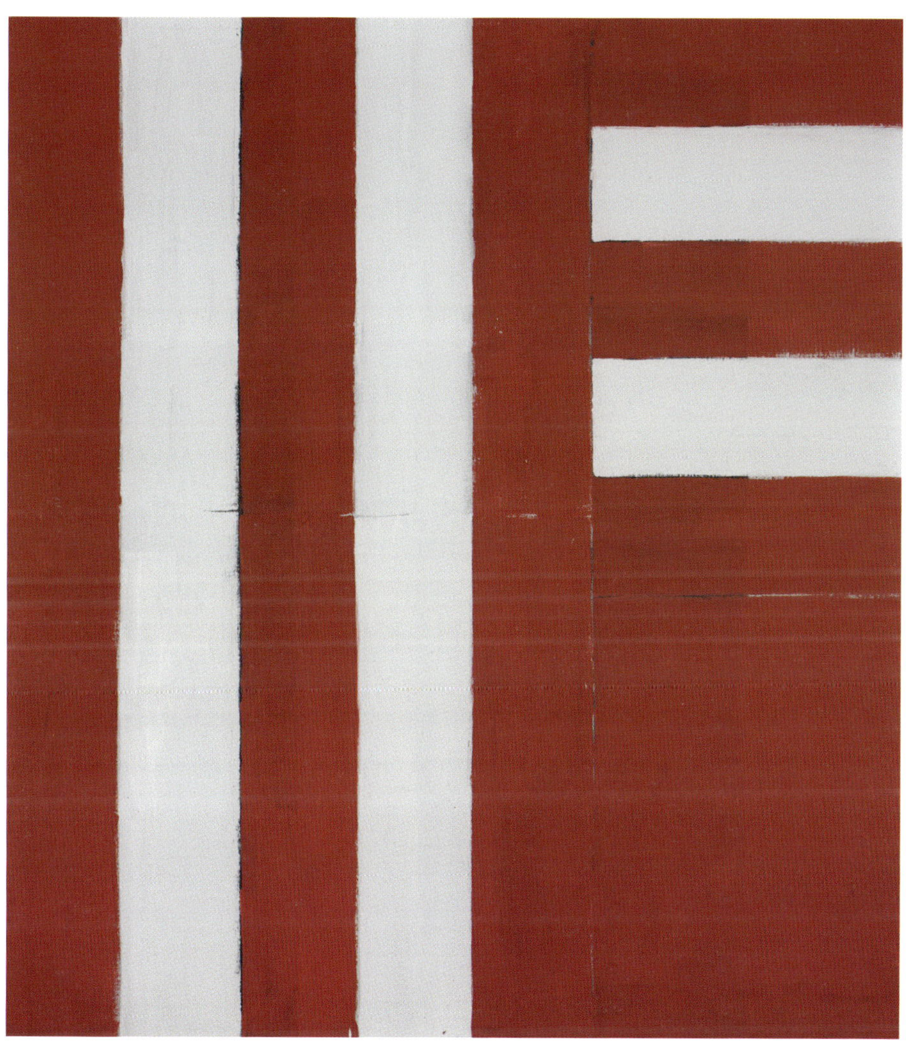

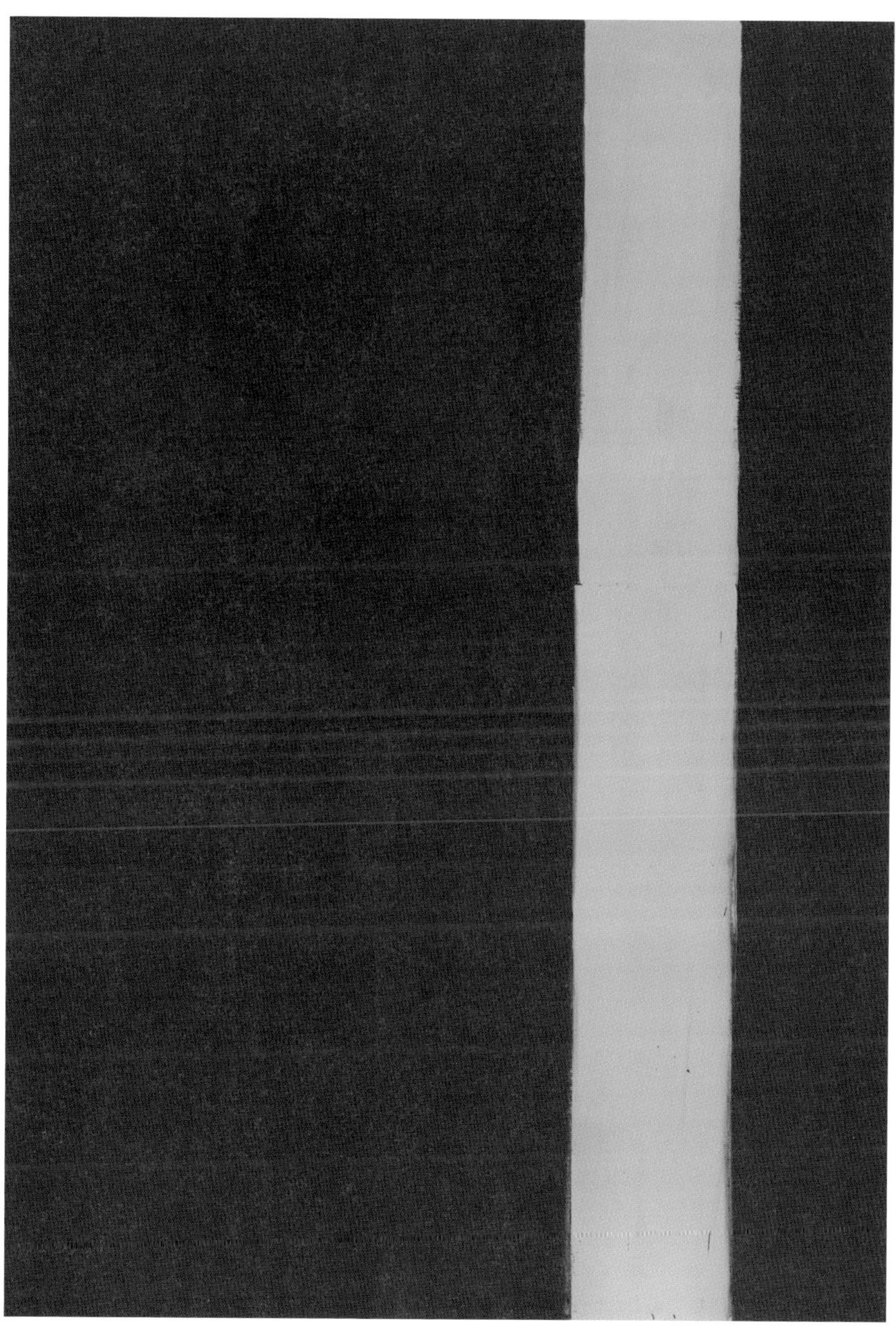

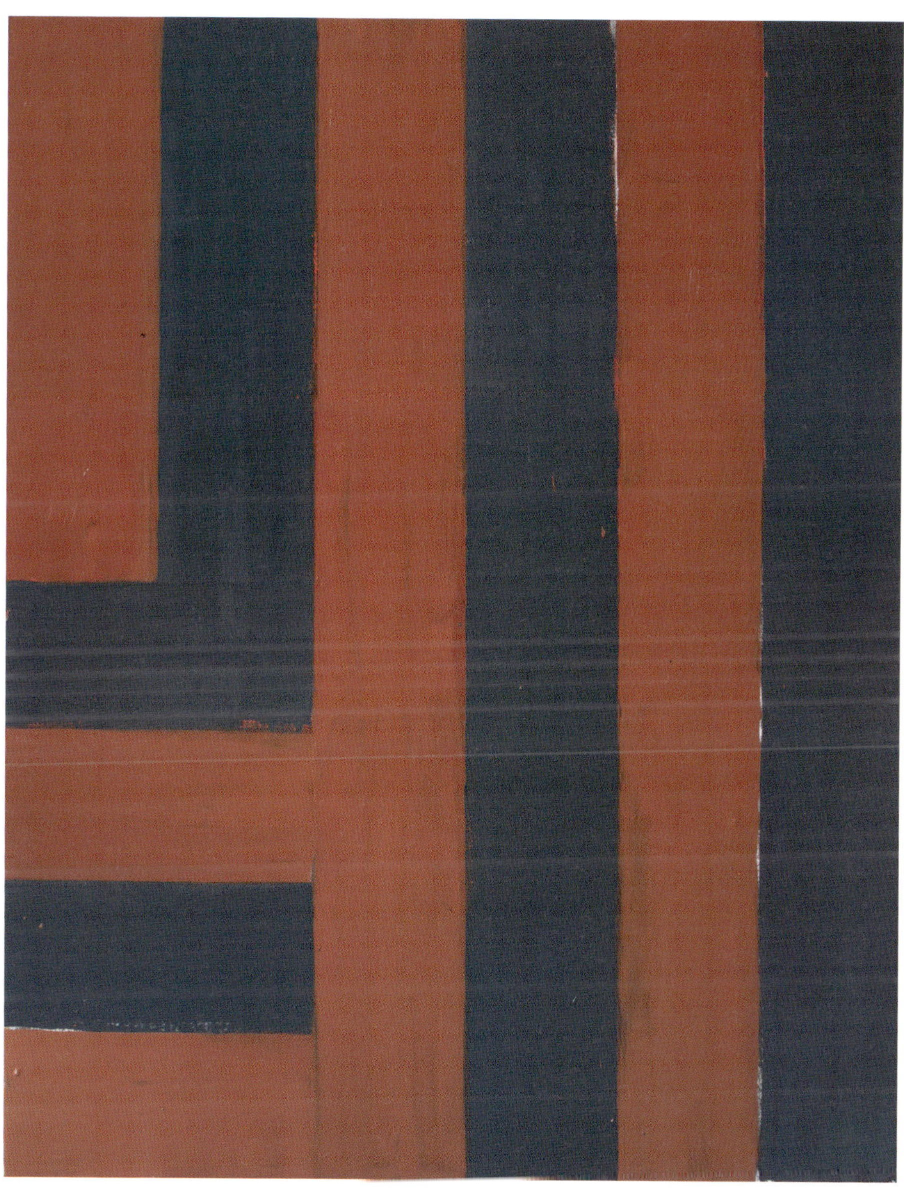

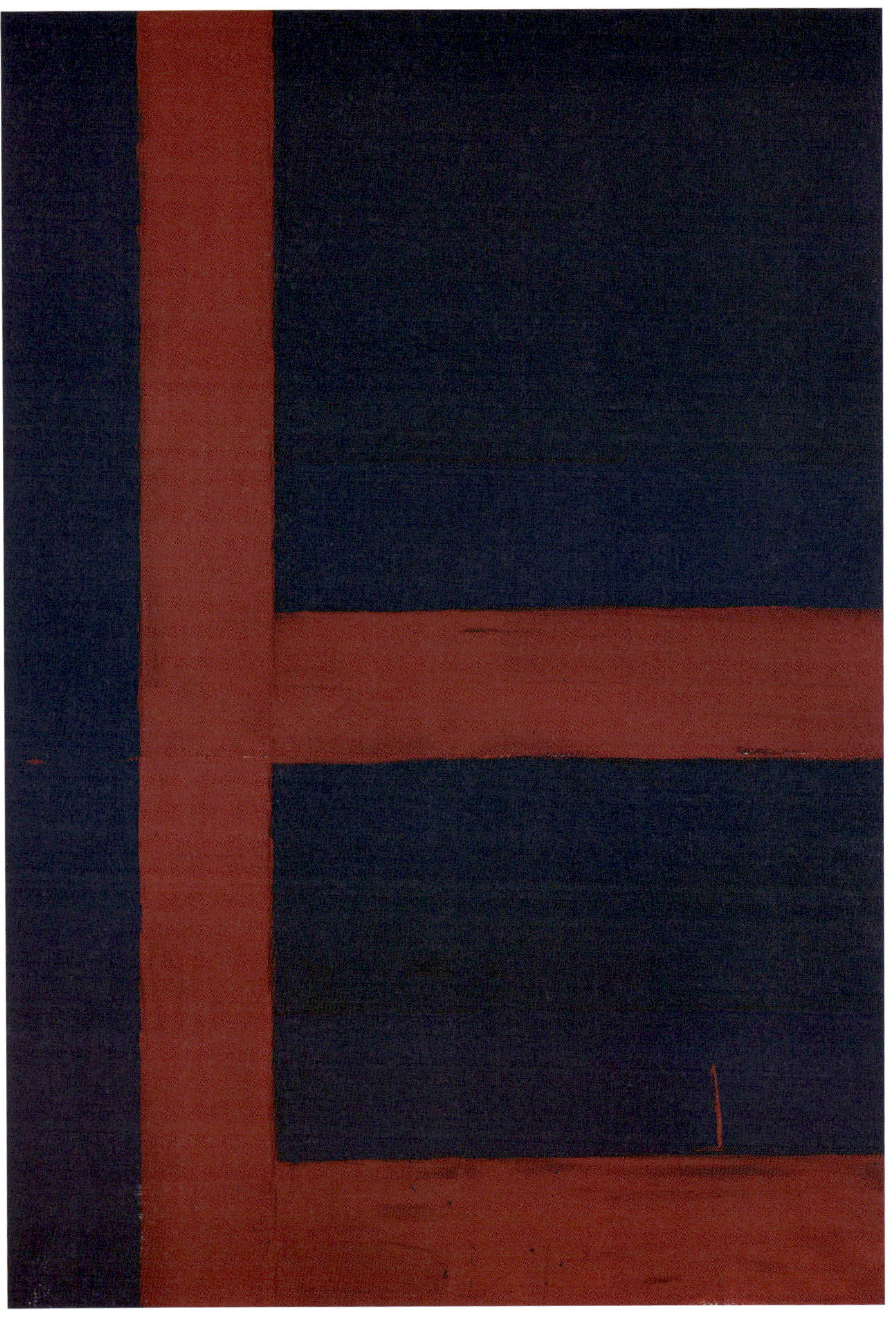

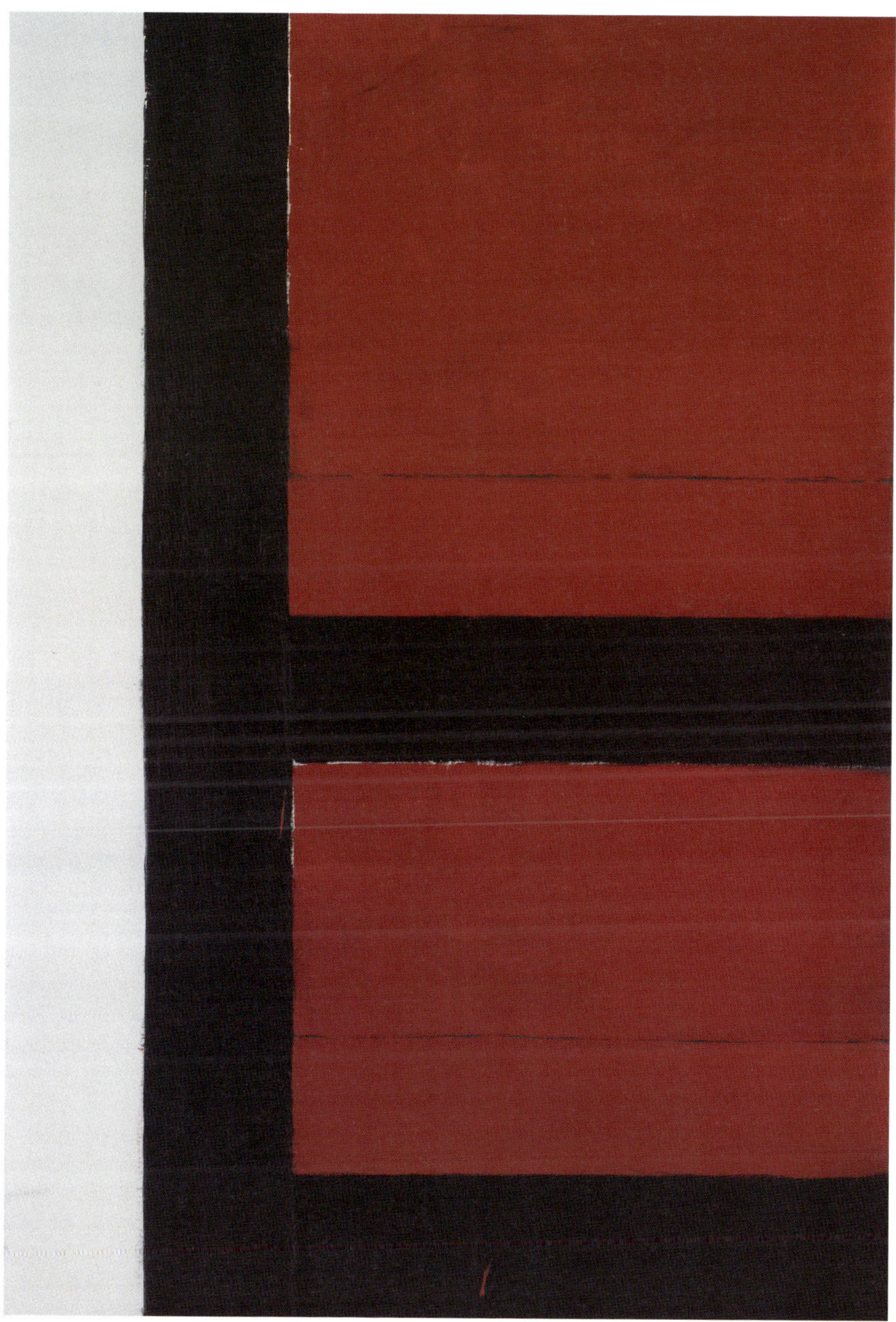

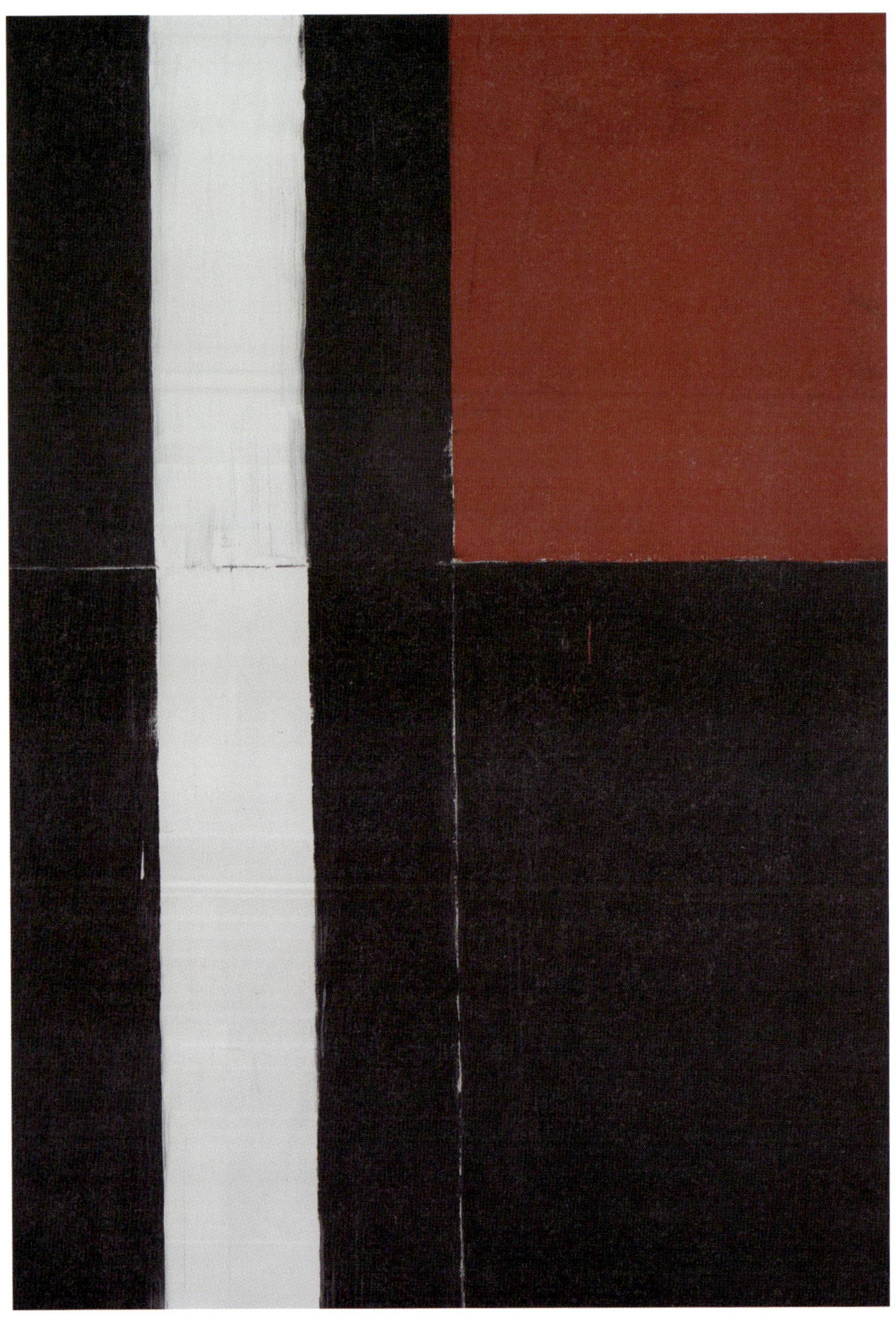

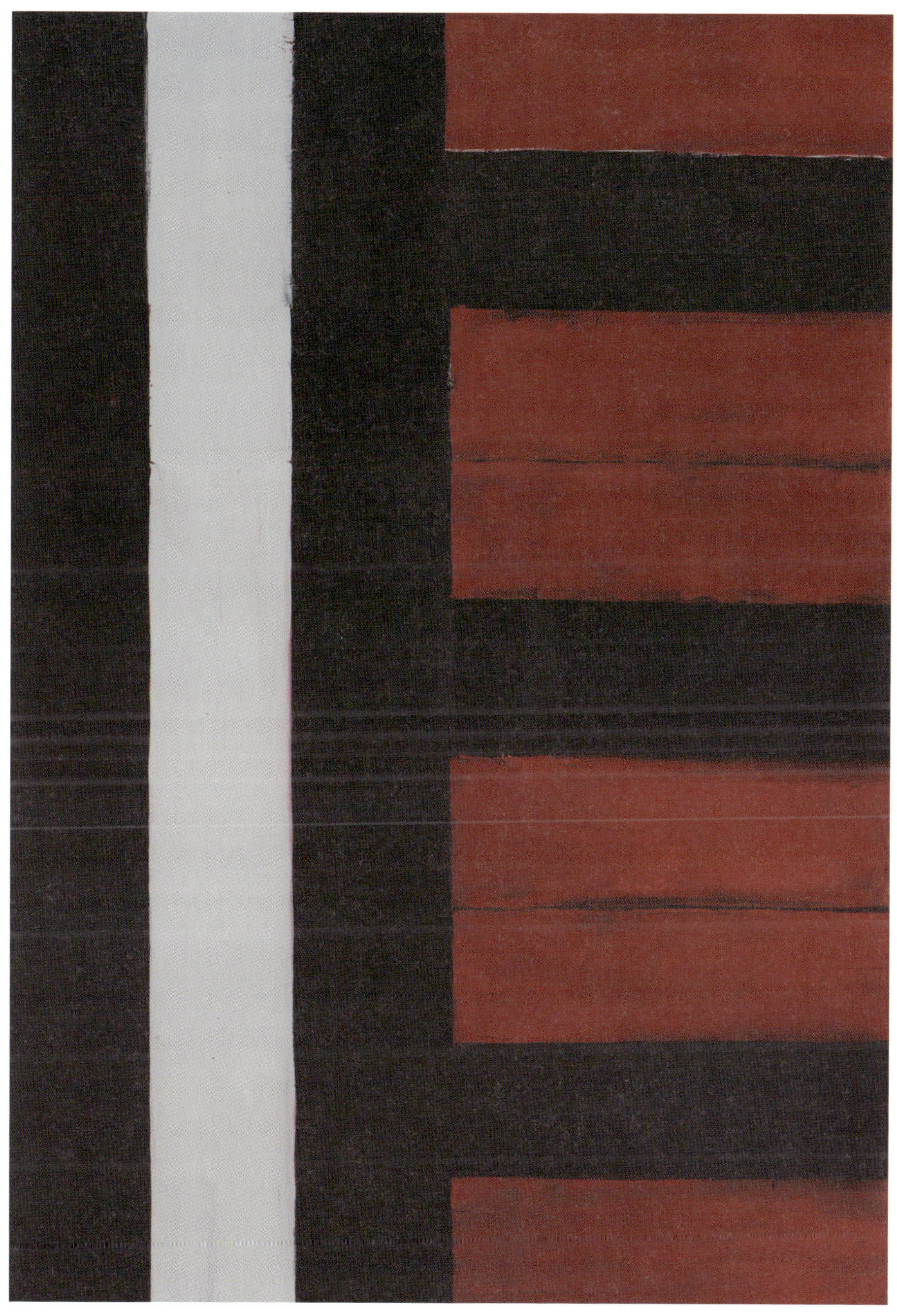

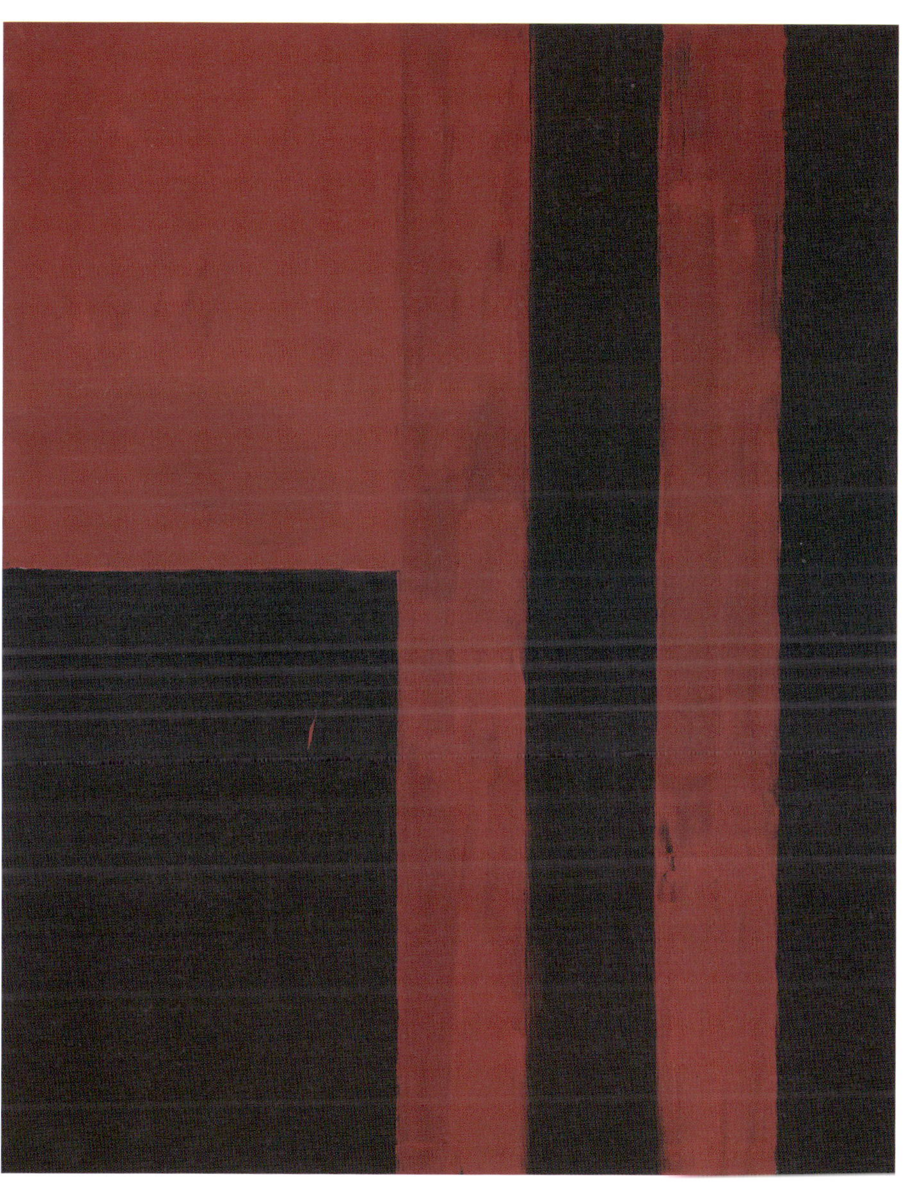

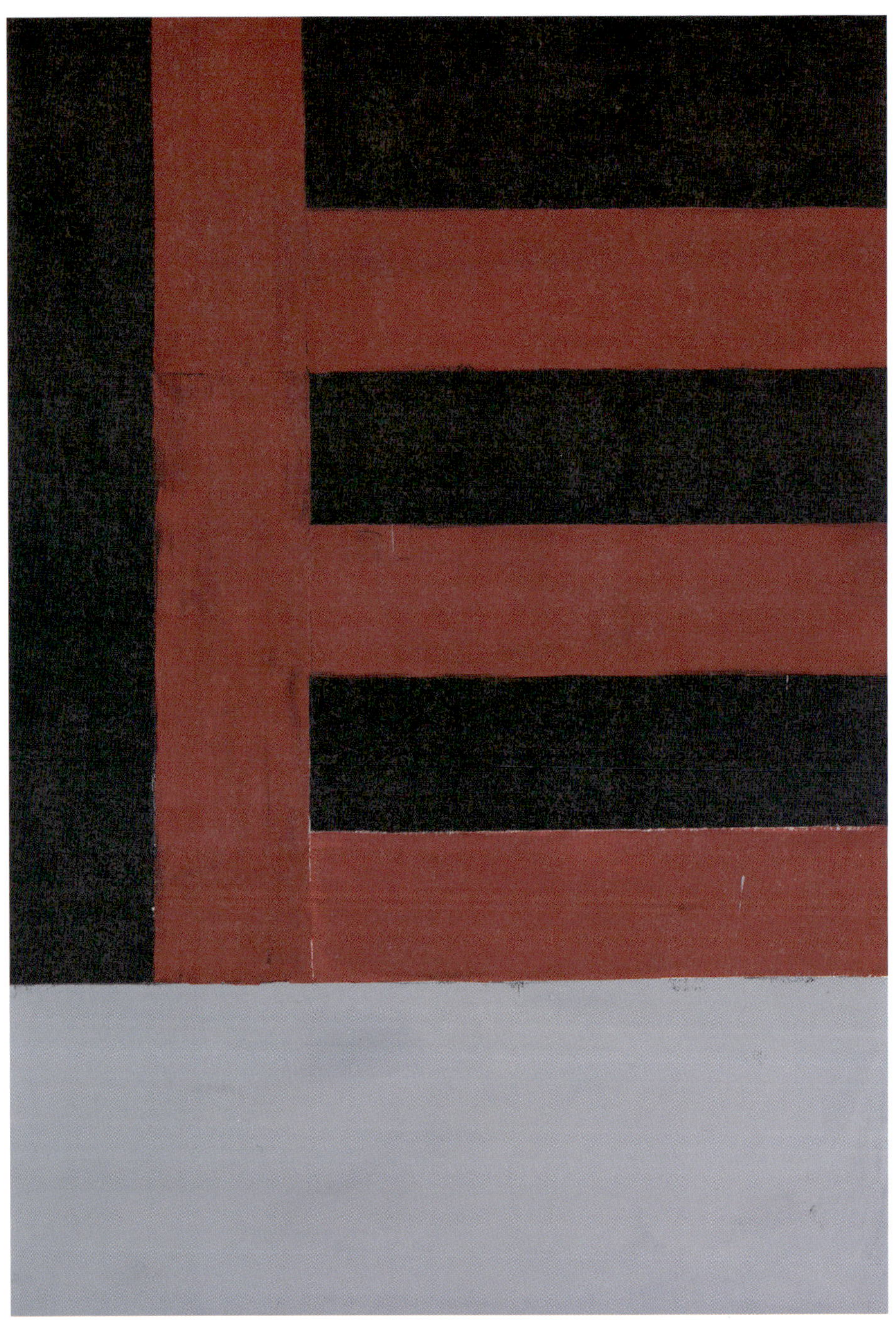

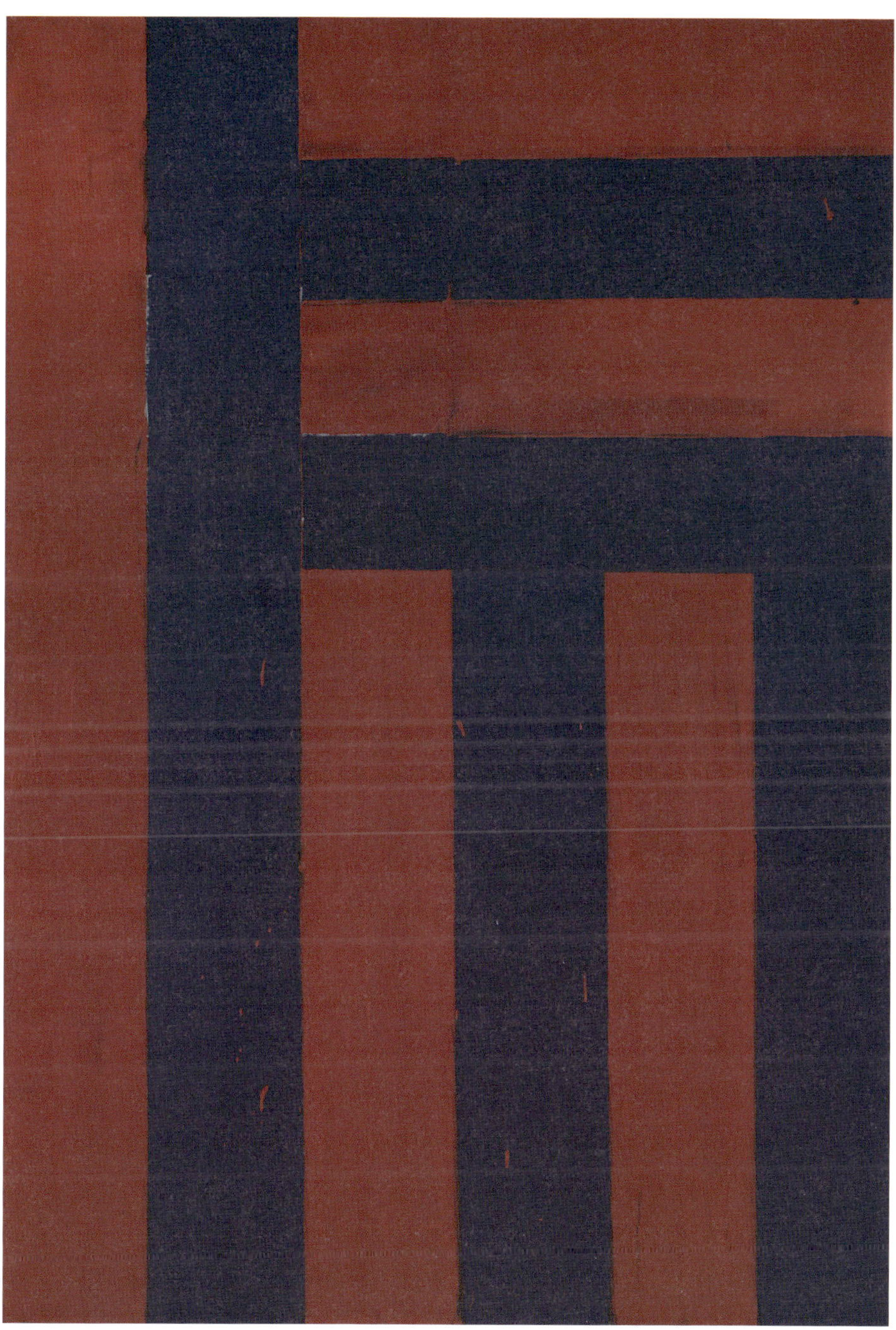

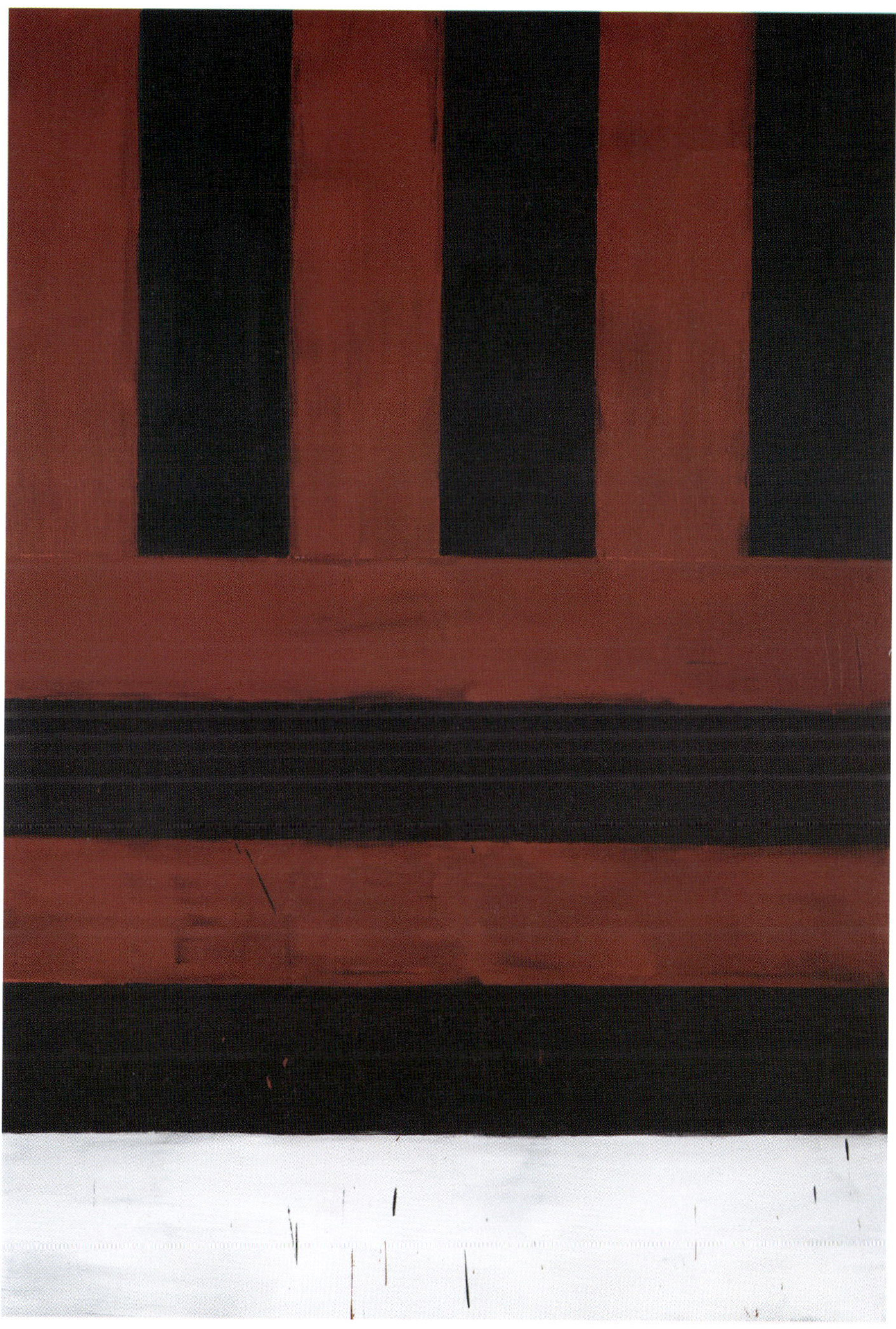

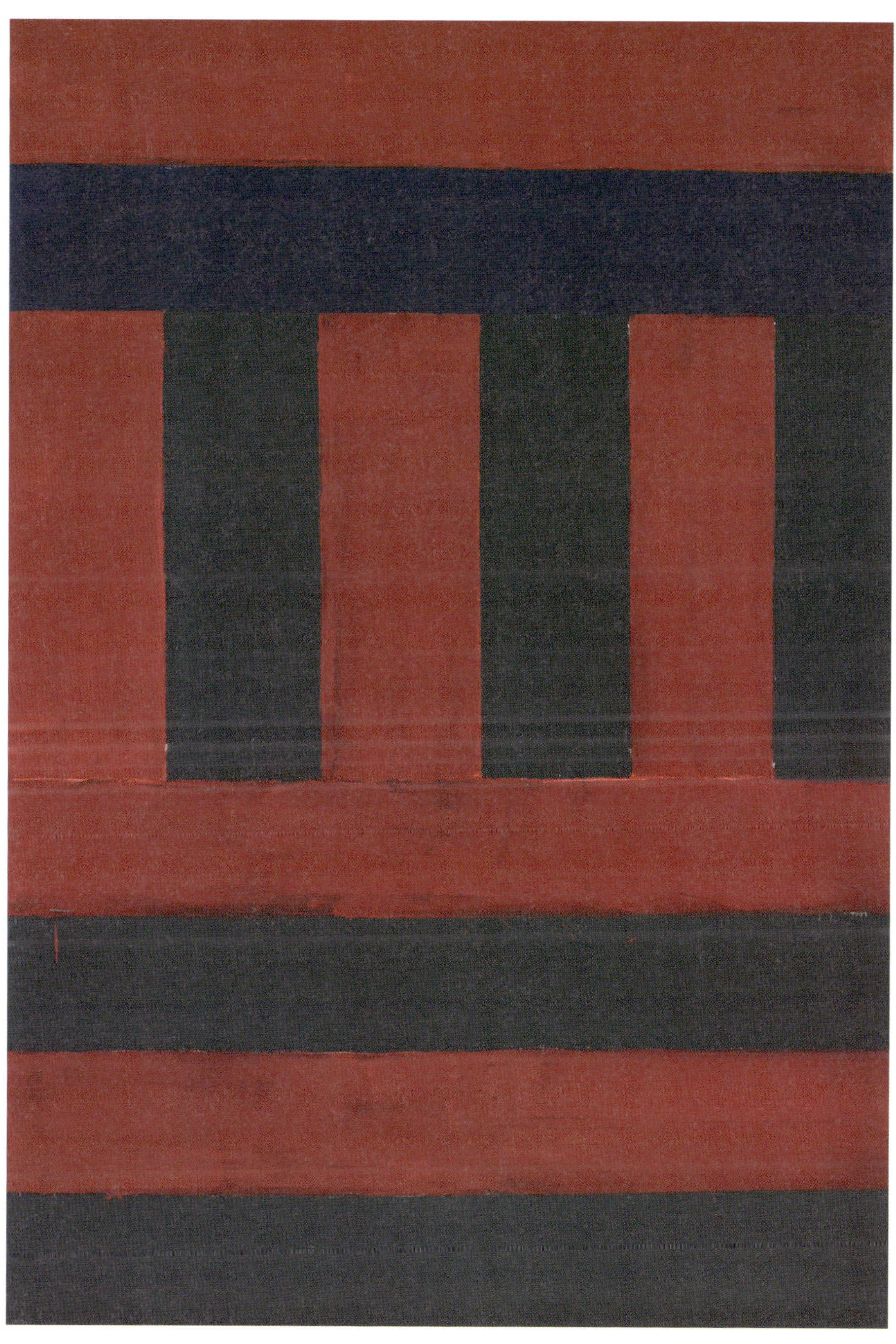

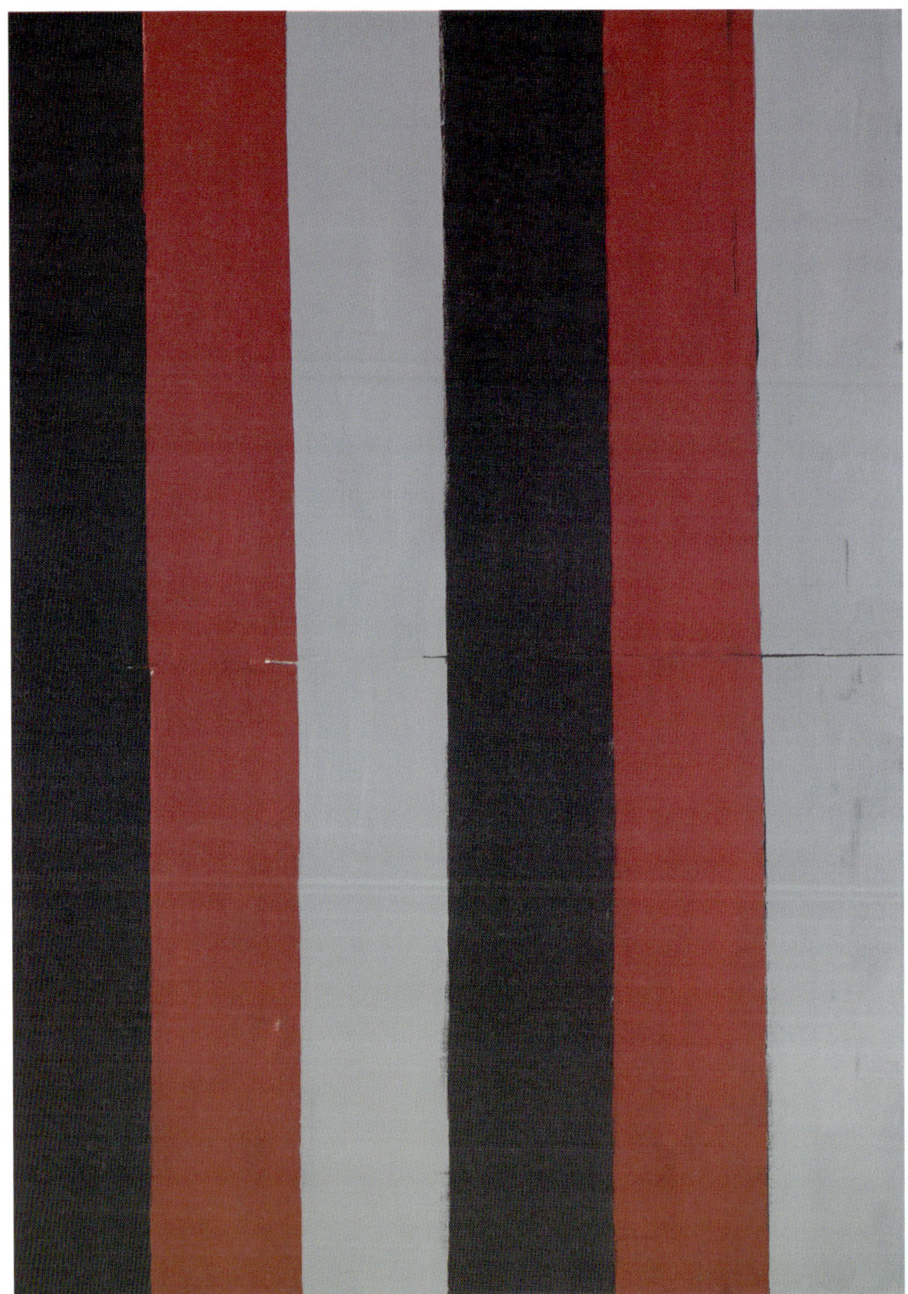

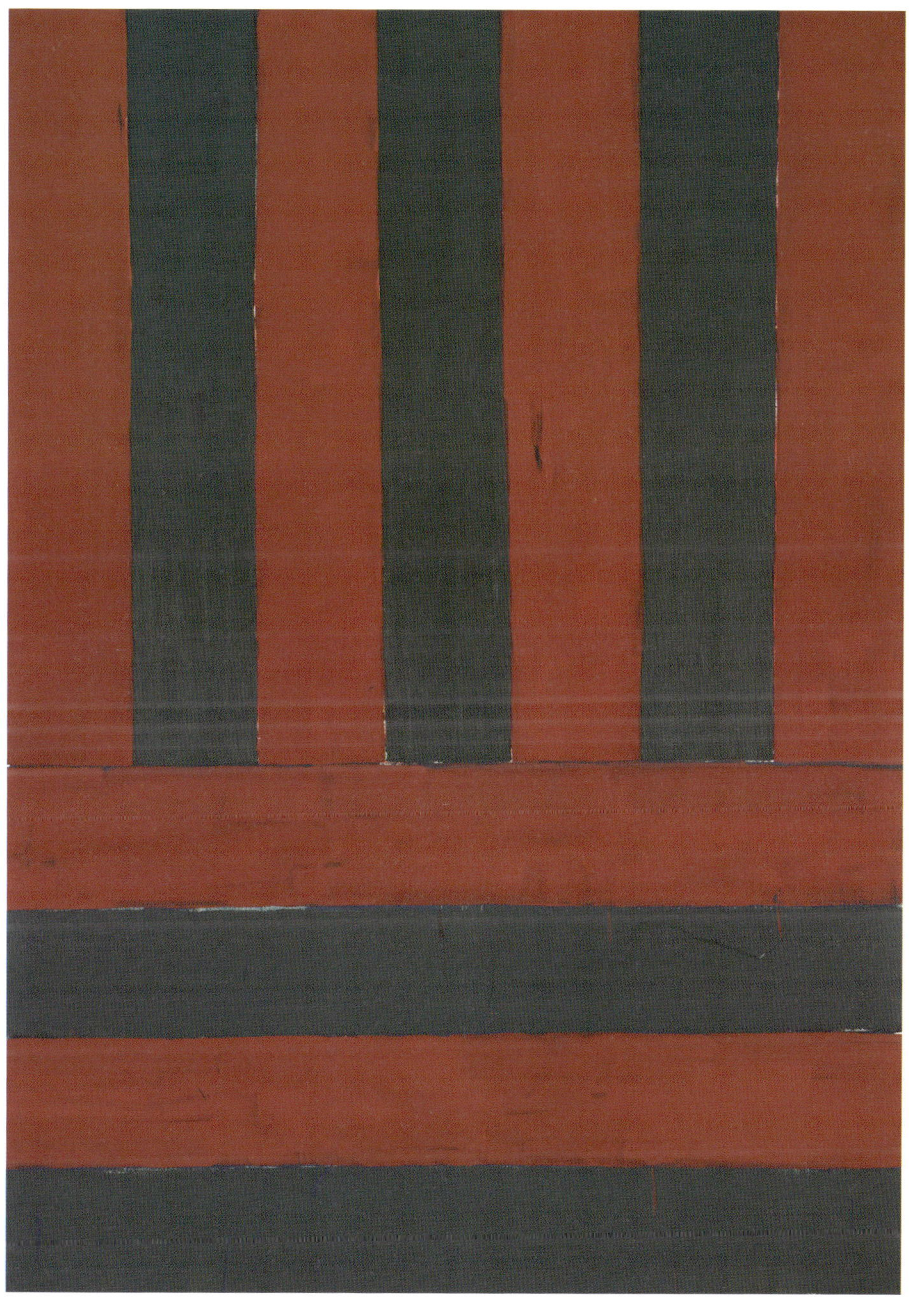

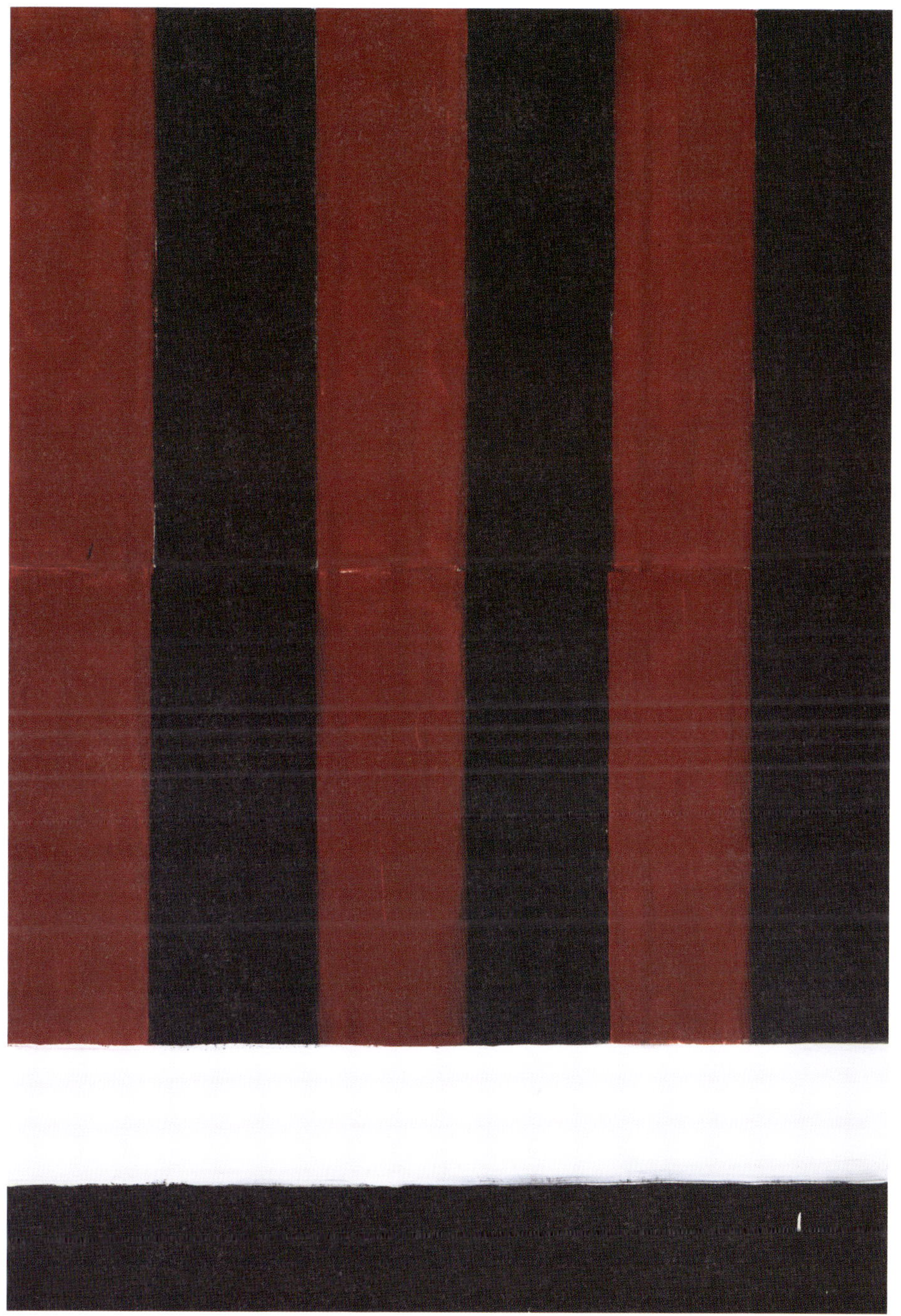

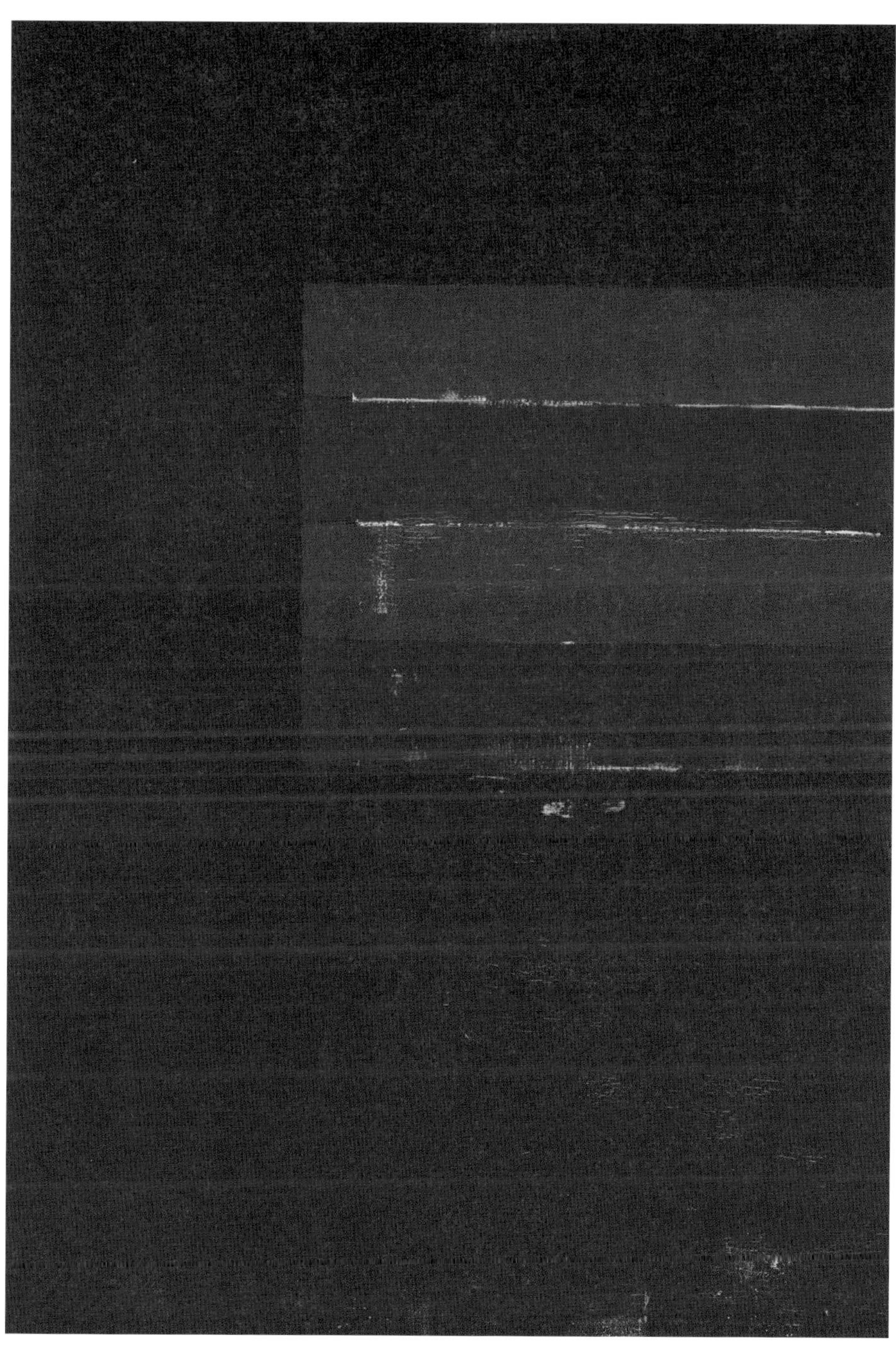

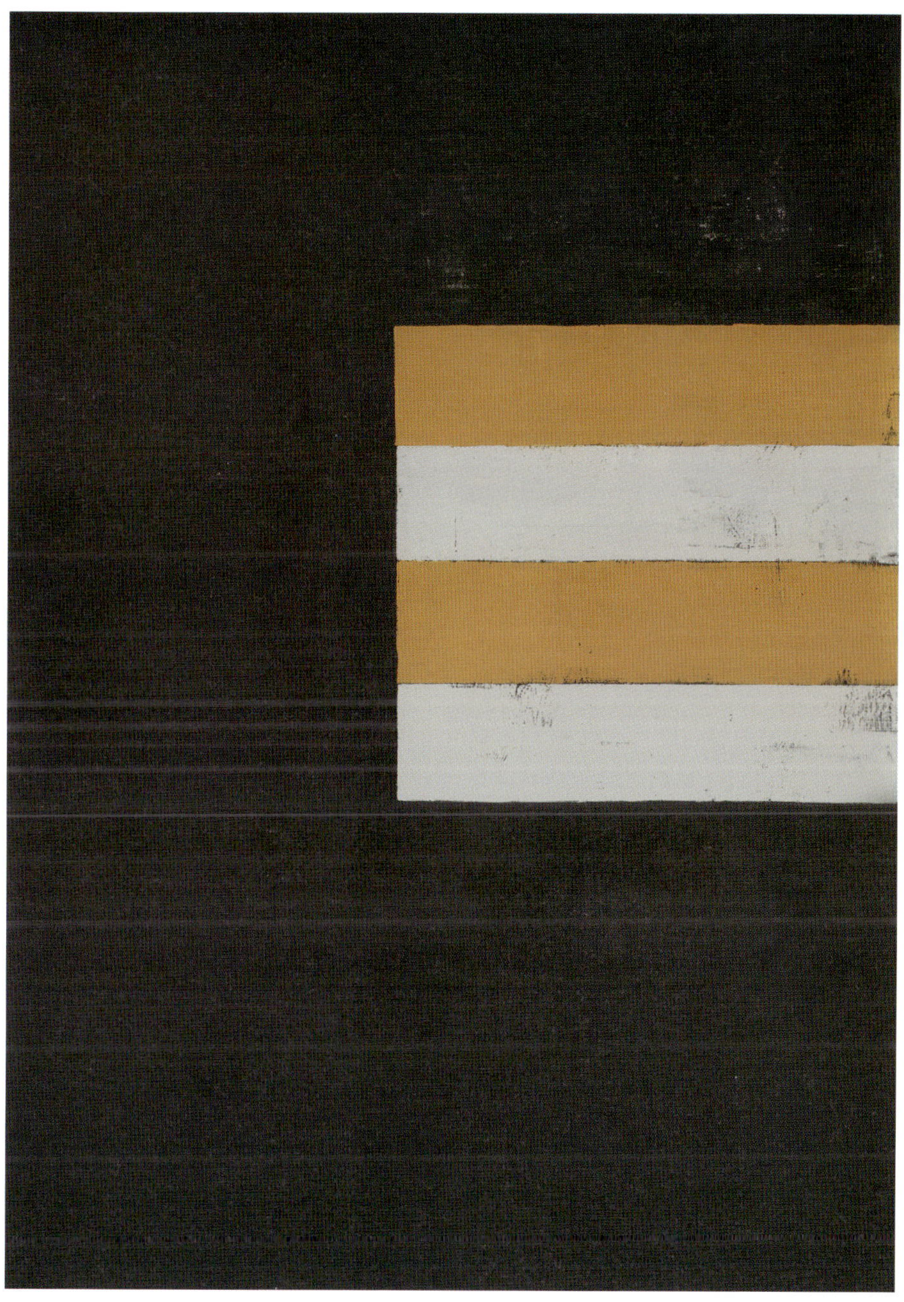

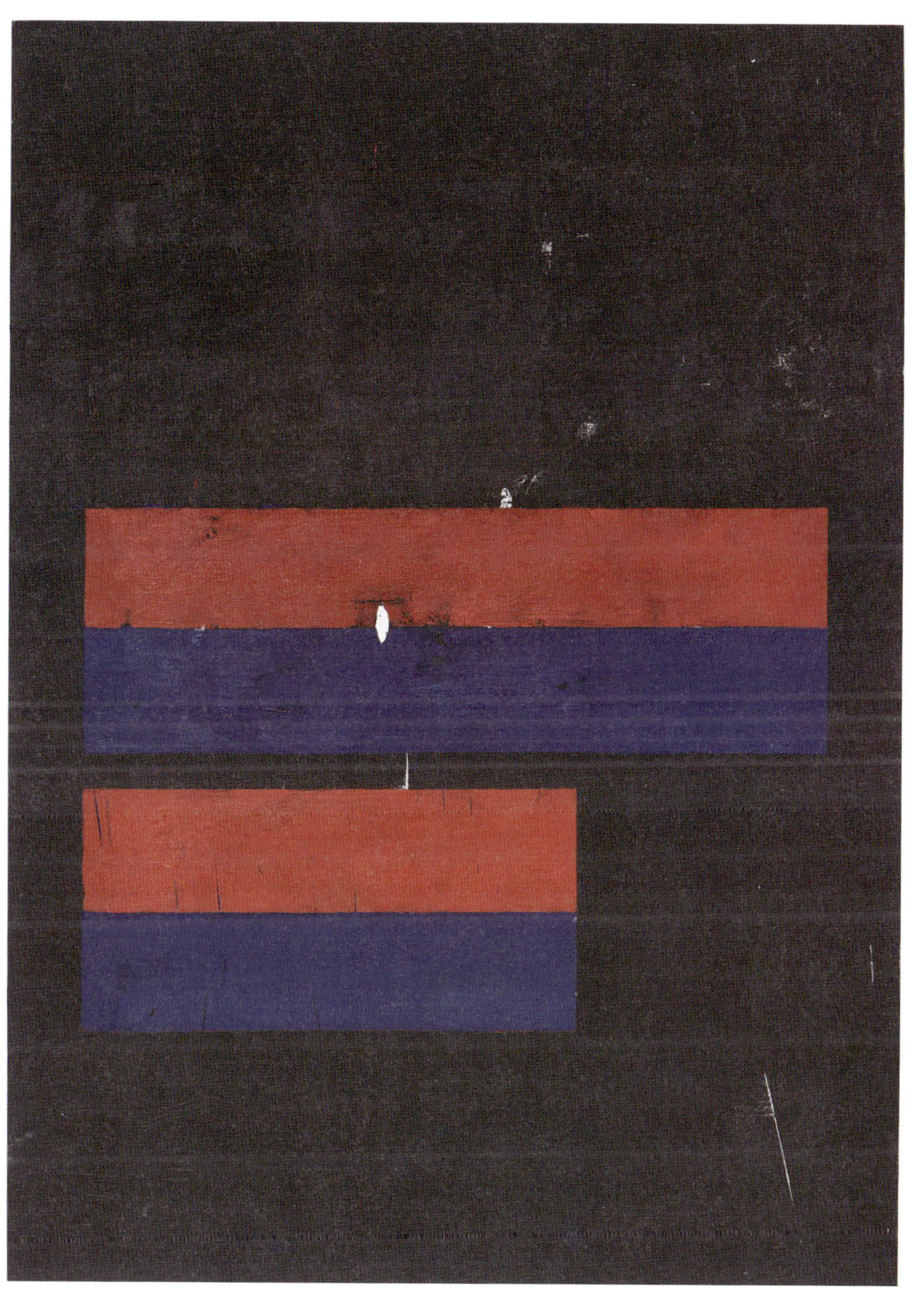

Nature Morte

Joseph Brodsky, 1971

Verrà la morte e avrà i tuoi occhi.
C. Pavese

I
People and things crowd in.
Eyes can be bruised and hurt
by people as well as things.
Better to live in the dark.

I sit on a wooden bench
watching the passers-by—
sometimes whole families.
I am fed up with the light.

This is a winter month.
First on the calendar.
I shall begin to speak
when I'm fed up with the dark.

II
It's time. I shall now begin.
It makes no difference with what.
Open mouth. It is better to speak,
although I can also be mute.

What then shall I talk about?
Shall I talk about nothingness?
Shall I talk about days, or nights?
Or people? No, only things,

since people will surely die.
All of them. As I shall.
All talk is a barren trade.
A writing on the wind's wall.

III
My blood is very cold—
its cold is more withering
than iced-to-the-bottom streams.
People are not my thing.

I hate the look of them.
Grafted to life's great tree,
each face is firmly stuck
and cannot be torn free.

Something the mind abhors
shows in each face and form.
Something like flattery
of persons quite unknown.

IV
Things are more pleasant. Their
outsides are neither good
nor evil. And their insides
reveal neither good nor bad.

The core of things is dry rot.
Dust. A wood-borer. And
brittle moth-wings. Thin walls.
Uncomfortable to the hand.

Dust. When you switch lights on,
there's nothing but dust to see.
That's true even if the thing
is sealed up hermetically.

V
This ancient cabinet—
outside as well as in—
strangely reminds me of
Paris's Notre Dame.

Everything's dark within
it. Dustmop or bishop's stole
can't touch the dust of things.
Things themselves, as a rule,

don't try to purge or tame
the dust of their own insides.
Dust is the flesh of time.
Time's very flesh and blood.

VI
Lately I often sleep
during the daytime. My
death, it would seem, is now
trying and testing me,

placing a mirror close
to my still-breathing lips,
seeing if I can stand
non-being in daylight.

I do not move. These two
thighs are like blocks of ice.
Branched veins show blue against
skin that is marble white.

VII
Summing their angles up
as a surprise to us,
things drop away from man's
world—a world made with words.

Things do not move, or stand.
That's our delirium.
Each thing's a space, beyond
which there can be no thing.

A thing can be battered, burned,
gutted, and broken up.
Thrown out. And yet the thing
never will yell, 'Oh, fuck!'

VIII
A tree. Its shadow, and
earth, pierced by clinging roots.
Interlaced monograms.
Clay and a clutch of rocks.

Roots interweave and blend.
Stones have their private mass
which frees them from the bond
of normal rootedness.

This stone is fixed. One can't
move it, or heave it out.
Tree shadows catch a man,
like a fish, in their net.

IX
A thing. Its brown color. Its
blurry outline. Twilight.
Now there is nothing left.
Only a *nature morte*.

Death will come and will find
a body whose silent peace
will reflect death's approach
like any woman's face.

Scythe, skull, and skeleton—
an absurd pack of lies
Rather: 'Death, when it comes,
will have your own two eyes.'

X
Mary now speaks to Christ:
'Are you my son?—or God?
You are nailed to the cross.
Where lies my homeward road?

Can I pass through my gate
not having understood:
Are you dead?—or alive?
Are you my son?—or God?'

Christ speaks to her in turn.
'Whether dead or alive,
woman, it's all the same—
son or God, I am thine.'

translated by George L. Kline

List of Works

All the works are *untitled*, and are in oil on canvas

10–11
2017, 200x140cm

12–13
2017, 200x180cm

14–15
2017, 200x140cm

17
2017, 200x160cm

19–27
2017, 200x140cm

29
2017, 200x160cm

30–35
2017, 200x140cm

36–37
2017, 250x180cm

39
2017, 200x140cm

40
2017, 180x150cm

41
2017, 200x140cm

43
2017, 200x150cm

44–49
2016, 200x140cm

51
2016, 250x180cm

52
2016, 200x140cm

53
2016, 250x180cm

55
2016, 200x200cm

56–57
2016, 200x140cm

59–61
2015, 200x140cm

62–63
2016, 250x360cm

64–65
2015, 200x270cm

67
2015, 250x180cm

69
2016, 200x140cm

70–71
2015, 200x250cm

73
2015, 250x180cm

75
2015, 250x180cm

76–77
2015, 200x270cm

79
2015, 200x140cm

82–83
2016, 250x180cm

Born in 1987 in Tighina (Bender), Moldova, Maxim Liulca studied at the *University of Art and Design in Cluj-Napoca* from 2005 to 2010. Among his latest solo shows are *Flags* in 2016 at Nicodim Gallery, Los Angeles (USA), *Was Sich Bezweit, Bedtritt Sich* in 2015 and *Paintings* in 2013 at Baril Gallery, Cluj-Napoca (RO). In 2015, *The right angle policy* at Anexa MNAC Bucharest (RO) and in 2014, *Bloom* at Spazio A Gallery, Pistoia (IT). He has taken part in several group exhibitions, such as *Layers*, in 2016 at Nicodim Gallery, Bucharest (RO), *Appearance and Essence* at the 2015 Art Encounters Biennale, Timisoara (RO). In 2014 *The Go-Between* at Museo Capodimonte, Napoli (IT) and *A Few Grams of Red, Yellow, and Blue* at Ujazdowsky Castle, Warsaw (PL).

Maxim Liulca thanks to:

Tiberiu Adelmann, Uta Grosenick, Jörg Johnen, Cătălin Lazurca, Daniel Marzona, Anna Olenicenco, Tanja Skorepa and Wilhelm Weiss (Strabag Kunstforum, Vienna), Rebecca Wilton

The book is published as part of the *Residence and Internship for Youngsters Programme* financed by *Centrul Municipal de Cultură Arad*

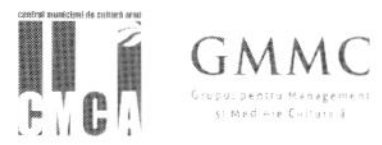

Colophon

Editor
:B A R I L Gallery
www.baril.ro

Concept and Design
Maxim Liulca

Texts
Maxim Liulca and Sorin Neamţu, 2017
Joseph Brodsky, *Nature Morte,* 1971

Translations
Lavinia Braniște (pages 5-8)
George L. Kline (pages 80-81)

Copy Editing
Rareș Moldovan

Photo Credits and Image Editing
Pavel Curagău / YAP Studio

Production Management
Cristina Coșorean, IDEA Print&Design

Production
IDEA Print&Design Cluj-Napoca, Romania

Distribution
Edel Germany GmbH
www.edel.com
distanz@edel.com

ISBN 978-3-95476-219-4
Printed in Romania

Published by
DISTANZ Verlag
www.distanz.de

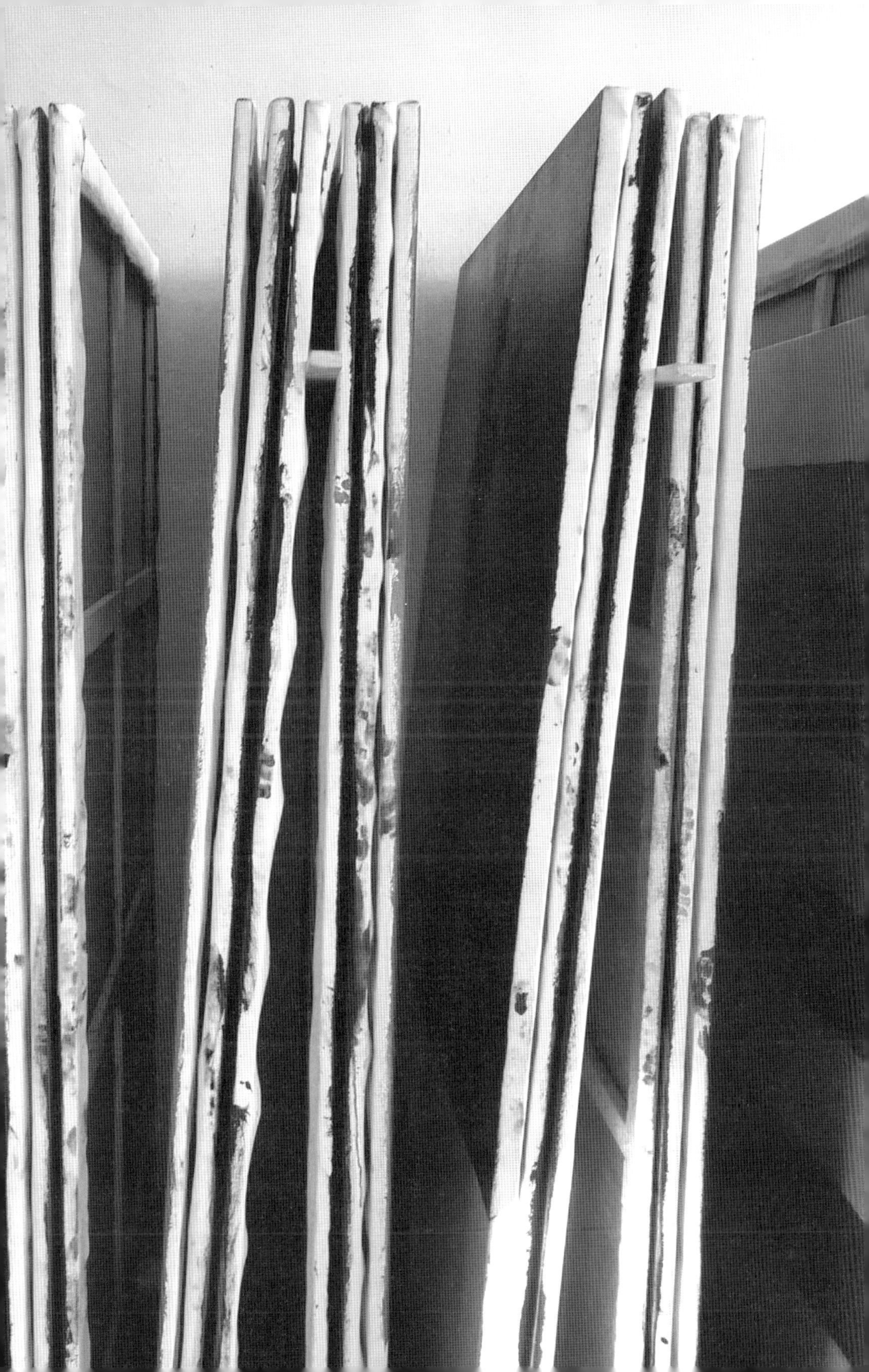